Also by Victor W. Pearn

Blame it on a Lightning Bolt

Swans Pausing

Pyromaniac

Dancing Bears

American Western Song: poems

Devil Dogs and Jarheads

Point Guard

Cryptozoology Poems

Postcard from Athens

*Dream Season: My Brother Gary and the
    1957 Ashland Panthers*

Light Across the Alley

Apricot Harvest

POEMS

Victor W. Pearn

INDIAN PAINTBRUSH POETS

COLORADO

Acknowledgments

Thanks to the editors of the following publications where these poems have previously appeared: Jining University newspaper in Qufu, China, (translated into Chinese); *The Coloradan; Muse International*.

Cover design by Anne Kilgore.

Indian Paintbrush Poets is an imprint of
Pearn and Associates, Inc., Book Publishing
1600 Edora Court Suite D
Fort Collins, Colorado 80525
For manuscript submission query by mail,
or email victorpearn@ymail.com.

Library of Congress Control Number: 2012938101

Pearn, Victor W.
Apricot Harvest, by Victor W. Pearn.
ISBN 978-0-9846523-7-2 paperback

Printed in the United States of America
Canada, United Kingdom, Europe and Australia

1st, edition.

For my wife Summer

Thank You

There are three people I want to thank because without their help *Apricot Harvest* could not have been written and published.

Thanks to George M. Eberhart, author of *Mysterious Creatures*, who bravely went into the Chinese Embassy at Chicago and hand-carried my passport to them for me, as my friend, so they would give me a visa to enter China. He also sent the passport with visa back to me in Boulder.

Thanks to Li Gang, the Director of the Foreign Language Department for creating a position for me to teach English at Jining University in Qufu, China.

And a special thanks to Michael Cooper my publisher for *Devil Dogs and Jarheads*, for persuading me to change my archaic publishing paradigm, and enabling me to publish this book with my own poetry imprint, Indian Paintbrush Poets.

Contents

Confucius Wall

Jining University Students

The Green Jade Flute

Home Again: An Epilogue

"The harvest is plentiful,

but the workers are few."

Luke 10

Confucius
Wall

Living Inside Confucius Wall

A few have lived here before
in peace and harmony
where moonlight still shines
brilliant orange in October haze.

And along Gu Lou street you may
hear the clomp clomping sound
of old horses pulling tourists
to and from the Confucius temple.

Here there are intricate
roof patterns and those
ancient eaves built to overlap,

fill in space, as if sky and eaves
were lovers, touching over and under.

Chinese

There is
a clear
innocence
about
the people
in China,
and a simple
beauty
in their language,
unlike any other
language.

A soft rain
fell all day.

It Wasn't Personal

A simple question
Fiona asked me,
"Could you write a poem
about teaching at a Chinese university?"

Flying, swimming, on
my way here—
one generation passes
their wisdom, accumulated
knowledge, and faith to another.

Oh and in conclusion, as
colorful as a magnificent Hawai'ian rainbow,
you learn to be creative, innovative,
and say, may I ask—why not?

In Fushun China

They scraped the deep snow
off the wide frozen river
in Fushun where many
speed skaters are skating.
They follow each other
every move duplicated perfectly.

Flying high above is
a red, white and blue kite that gives me hope.
There are many ice skaters
and kite fliers here.
Today my *fiancée* and I have waited
eighteen days to get our wedding papers stamped.

Far overhead in
that brilliant blue
a long white cloud is billowing;
from a power plant's tall thin smokestack
the cloud rises across space like
a vacant dragon, threatening
to swallow the sun.

Neon Lights

They are building sixty story slums
all over China.

You can catch the bus
one hour standing,
and everywhere
looks the same.

People in China
copy and imitate things,
but they make bad copies
and poor product imitations.

I had expected to be impressed
with fantastic gardens.
What I've found was
rotten pollution,
dirty air. And water
so bad it must be boiled
before you can drink it.

They really do need to do better.

Like fireflies shining in unison above a bayou,
neon lights flash an amazing light show
on bridges and buildings everywhere.

Apricot Harvest

You can go home
and wait, or
you may possibly
meditate beside
the Jade Green River.

Confucius planted
his apricot trees
on this riverbank in Qufu.
I love apricots.
We share a simple taste.

Pegasus

The landscape is depressing with
poverty in the countryside.
People work hard for little wages.
Even the *value of money* is poor.
Today red lanterns
are snow capped.
Basketball sized lanterns hung
along the streets were the New Years'
ornaments; symbolic
of good luck.
I saw an amazing
white Pegasus
rearing up with wings spread wide.
Perhaps Pegasus will carry us home.

This Old Place

Stone, iron, pillars, beams, here—
these are Chinese artifacts.
A column reaching up to the stars
was standing guard for an ancient tomb.

Well the old New Orleans Saints won
a Super Bowl.
The Who played for the Saints at half-time.
A surprise onside kick for the win.
And they had a fireworks show.

Hu Jin Tao is the Chinese President.
A mysterious set of coincidences.

All night here in Qufu
loud explosions and fireworks
go off outside the bedroom window.
And it really was in the year of the tiger.

Corn Stacks and Beggars

An old man is hauling hard corncobs at harvest.
He has a white stringy chin beard.
He's a very poor farmer.
There aren't any rice paddies here.
Corn was spread out over the roads
for traffic to run over and smash and
separate the hard kernels from cobs.
And great corn stalk stacks
stand far across the long field.
There isn't any democracy or freedom around.
These red lanterns are everywhere
for the Lunar New Years' celebration,
and those red knots are for luck.
Also along the many wide and narrow streets are
old beggars that need food and medicine.

A New Lunar Year

Thinking I might have a bad cold,
eyes were tearing up
I was sneezing and my nose was dripping,
it was a reaction to the irritants
in the smoke filled sky.

February 13, people
stayed up shooting bombs,
at midnight I went out
to see the chaotic mess.
The fireworks explosions were astonishing.

More than being thrust into
a hazardous combat zone,
roman candles and large bombs were bursting
everywhere, ignited by citizens.
It was sad to witness
a billion dollars worth of flashes gone up
in poisonous puffs of smoke.

I imagined some grand hospital,
with that kind of money,
help for poor farmers, or
universities with heated classrooms.

Tiger Tiger Burning Bright

There are fifty or less
wild tigers living free in the peoples republic.
Tigers bring good luck,
as do dragons and red lanterns.
Real tigers are very endangered
a species at risk here,
although gold tigers, and images
are everywhere this year.
In Weihai at a seafood restaurant
you order living food in the outer room.
Choose your dinner. Anything endangered
you can afford. National TV ads ask people
to stop buying.
Any food may be served;
Chinese enjoy these wild dishes.

Tiananmen Square

We treated ourselves
to a small taxi tour from Lucky Street
around infamous
Tiananmen Square.

We went past the place
where Mao Tse-tung was entombed.
Also we drove by an enormous
entrance to the Great Wall of China.

Jasmine Jazz

Entertainment and showing fashions
are important here.
There are many concerts and
performers dance or sing one number
to an audience of thousands.

Performances are broadcast
on national TV
and younger entertainers
imitate Michael Jackson
wearing much out of place gang clothing.

They dance and sing rap music
in their own language,
a warped and funhouse mirror
imitation of American rap with
light shows and fireworks in the backdrop.

Amazing because there was
a pretty good jazz singer
that performed one song
accompanied by an authentic band;
a jasmine jazz oasis.

Jining
University
Students

Primitive

On the street and in
some shops stretched hides
were for sale
skins and furs
hanging like the buffalo hides
did in the wild west.

Used for blankets
or rugs with painted fake
striped tigers or spotted
leopards, many unsuspecting
gullible souls buy these
thinking they bought the real thing.

But the little black nose
and the little pointed ears left on
those hides were from
some poor dog.
I find it primitive and an appalling
facet of another society in denial.

Beginning to Change

Old man winter
packs a bag and is leaving;
the bitter chill is gone.
The students and I have survived
these winter classrooms with no heat in them.
There is too much poverty.
The poor spread across the land,
you could look, or may want to
see it from the fast train.
Every place has dirt and run down houses.
Oh, the Nouveau riche
are dressed in the latest fashions;
they are buying silver and gold and
expensive cars, anything for show.
Water is neither potable, nor palatable.
Air is polluted with coal and nuclear waste.
All the students say China is
unquestionably beautiful.

The Lost Forest

A painter says
I will be sixty
in five years and
I worship trees.
I will make sixty paintings
one a month for five years
of trees by my sixtieth birthday.

The great trees
of China are
extinct, cut down
long ago,
millions of new thin trees
have been planted like poles everywhere
in even rows and
huddled like hungry masses too close together.
There aren't any natural
wilderness areas or anything
resembling a forest.

Fat Rat

My wife and I were in a restaurant
and this big rat ran up.
It leaped three times on the window sill,
fell each time
and ran back the way it came.
The waiters looked and laughed, and looked
and laughed.
I am losing weight.

Words for My Shandong Students

Look at the billowing cumulus clouds
and watch the purple martins fly.
Students, you are learning a new living language.
I believe in you.
There's nothing you cannot either accomplish or do.
The doors of the world have become
widely opened for you.

Metaphor Café
found lines in class 1

A four leaf clover.

A life with felicity
every leaf is comforting
with coffee
you may have happy thoughts.

The freshness of deep spring
lives forever in my heart
luck
and bright hope
in a clear sky with flowers.

The sun slants through the window
shining warmly
it brings you
love, glory, health, riches and
God is blessing you.

Who can see the future?
Love stands in my circle.
Happiness follows my shadow.
Luck kisses my shoulder.
A line between two hands,
life is like honey, golden and sweet.
A funny lazy teddy bear.

Love comes with subtle fragrance
lives peacefully beside the hot coffee cup
shines under the summer sun and
brings me back to my golden childhood.

An early morning
wandering the path,
I found a four leaf clover
swaying in the wind.
Maybe it was the one appearing in my dream,
reaching out to it for fortune,
and for felicity.
What is the meaning of life?
Look at it. Think about it.
Green life in the clover leaf will give you courage.
You can create your future.

Sip coffee, enjoy the adventure, the aroma,
taste the flavor and enjoy your life.
Look for happiness with a friend's calm heart and enjoy
coffee together.

The first clover leaf brings you love.
The second leaf flies you home on spring winds.
The third brings your desired halo.
The fourth carries you up into heaven.

Simile County
found lines in class 2

A gentle rain fell.

On the grass
the world
onto our hearts
light and softly.

And dancing on the leaves,
the wind like silk, touches
your elegant, peaceful, face.
The Yangtze flows through this ancient country
telling us its history is mysterious.
A fascinating reflection in the drizzly rain
as if hearing a murmuring voice.

Washing and brightening everything
in the rain and a mild breeze was
swaying the leaves of grass
I was pacing
lonely and depressed, but as I
listened to the song in the rain
my heart gradually regained peace.

An angel flew onto the earth
on that precious night.
You say our story is beginning.
The rain is a lovely witness:

it looks like a string of pearls,
sounds like leaping notes,
it kisses the grass, flowers, leaves,
and the thirsty earth,
like a child returning to a mother's embrace.
How gentle. How charming to
smash the gloom into pieces,
and then the sun shines
warm, peaceful, harmonious.
An earthquake destroys homes, but
strengthens souls;
I pray for a brighter day. Look
a wandering couple is surrounded by love,
hope, and happiness that will live forever.

So poetic, so sweet, so cool,
rain patter on windows is like joyful notes
in tune with the wind.
I walked in the rain listening
and let the rain touch me.

Pixilated Worse for Wear
found lines in class 5

If I can see the future
 I will speak less and think more.
If I can see the future
 I'll try my best to achieve my dreams.
If I can see the future
 I'll save resources to protect earth.
If I can see the future
 I'll ardently say I love you to family and friends.
If I can see the future
 I'll cherish what I have before doomsday.
If I can see the future
 what I'll do is struggle today.

Night is like tears of shooting stars, you said,
but you do not know how sad I was that night.
Please cherish me gently like you would treat flowers.

I'll cultivate love's seed in my garden.
I'll say love is patient and kind: not money, not fame.
I'll protect you forever with my wings.
I'll work hard for my own dreams, and
I'll see what life you make for yourself.

Please see what my future is like:
I'll cherish what I have achieved;
and I'll strive for better hopes.
If I can see the future
    I'll forget sad tears and sorrows,
and I'll work harder on my dreams.
I believe the future is bright, and sunshine
will shine on everyone's face.
I would like to unblind my eyes
and work the hardest looking at mysteries in life.
If I can see the future
    I will stop disasters from coming into the world,
and let flowers bloom all around.

I hope our world will be peaceful.
I wish for everyone to live a happy life.
I hope children grow in an harmonious atmosphere.
I won't ask life for too much, only for more love.

I'll be unique, confident, tenacious,
pursuing dreams, traveling the world.
I want to know what each day will be.
I'll ask God to bless China all the time too.
I hope our environment will become fresh,
and harmony will flourish on the earth.

Pushing Against Walls
found lines in class 6

Freedom is:
breaking the gaps
between countries and organizations;
struggling for rights and dreams
against all difficulties; just like
pushing against walls.
The biggest happiness for
a prisoner is freedom.

Going where you want to go.
Doing what you want to do.

A bird flying out of a cage,
the sky becoming bluer,
freedom is as important as air.

It is clear water spouting from fountains,
thoughts and memories that come floating
in like a riptide.
A river in the desert
giving powerful hope
a deep feeling.

A beautiful flower,
a wind softly touching your face,
ripe wheatfields to the horizon,
a silky wind through sycamore leaves,
leaves trembling on their branches,

or snowflakes drifting down;
a white cloud floating
in the brilliant sky.
The song
we are singing
one of the greatest gifts
we have been given,
we are free in life to think
to feel and to speak,
we are free in what we do
rejoice in your freedom.

It is the moment you realize
you can do whatever you want,
and you can travel around the world.

Freshman Year
found lines in class 7

Better dreams, better future,
love is the main topic. Look for dreams on the way. Bring
wonderful dreams into God's subtle heaven, new hopes are
like beautiful flowers in sunshine
believe and life's road will be opening up for you.
Angelic music approaches from the stars.

With the joy of studying
live a happy life
try your best
to achieve your ambitions
believe that one day
your dreams will come true,
blooming and fading
visualize growth
just like the sun
radiating from the clouds recently,
love shines in all places
I can feel it in you.

Bold energetic students
are a confident ambitious generation
like nature coming to life in spring,
they are active and as fresh
as flowers washed by rain,
like birds all year long

who will sing all their days
on the rough country roads,
this is who we are we're freshmen.

Affable, intelligent students,
coming from every geographical direction
happy together here;
dreams are sailing,
enthusiasm rising
through perilous peaks, or dangerous rivers,
ambition is strong,
we never give up, never say die.

Remember everyday
no matter how the day is
happy or sad
cherish your fondest dreams
sailing.

Share ideals from different places.
You come across at this golden time
becoming part of a global family,
be firm, just and true;
be sweet and virtuous. Your souls belong to you
and they shall never die.
Sing and dance together
your days are filled with sweet fragrant roses
flourishing early and abundantly in June.

Flowing Lava
found lines in class 3

Violent volcano eruptions, glaciers are melting
sea level is rising
the weather becomes warmer and warmer
our life is threatened
it is time to do something.

The earth is quaking crazily
the dinosaurs are extinct
I'm like wind flying here and there
the birds are singing
the gardenias are blooming
jade flute sounds surrounds us
and summer is coming.

The sun is rising, and darkness is going
time is changing, space is changing everything
is changing except my love for you.
Our hearts will go on.

Fire interweaves water
as lava flows into the Pacific
with yelling and shouting
all these things are frightening
if you leave me aside,
then it is the end of the world.

Passion in a volcanoes heart breaks fantastically,
power of glaciers, silently explored,

it is terrible, but it brings something new.
Flowing lava is going to form a beautiful jade flute.
It is not the end of the world in the year 2012,
believe and tomorrow comes on time.
Sunshine, melody, new hope, all approach followed by new
lava flowing.

Facing the sky
flying by night, it
never feels lonely
accompanied with spring
wind, it loves the land so deeply,
anxious but excited lava
cannot go far, and
you never know when it will come again.

Terrible earthquakes attack, and floods are flowing
God tell me, what makes you so angry?
Oh, is this world coming to an end? I wonder,
whatever lies underneath the shelter of nature,
my heart will go on living forever.

Even though
buildings are in ruins
numberless friends have passed by
rainbows were born
and Noah's Ark appeared;
everything will rest in silence and in
brilliance from sunshine. After the rain
I shall present this poem to survivors,
friends in disaster areas.

Summer's Honey Breath
found lines in class 4

Wind mildly touches flowers
as if they were smiling at you now
being happy in mid air and
breathing freely
as if they were fairies.

Oh China, how you are a developing culture.
So you have a long way to go
since you have chosen a distant place,
you are never stopped by
either rain or wind.

After spring rains flourish
crops are eager for summer irrigation.
Your country, your home, your childhood,
they all flowered in daylight.
The painted boat, the pale clouds,
the Milky Way, the herons flapping their wings,
words fail to portray this scene.

You are heading toward
a brilliant future.
Walking ahead steadily
every season, every night is lively
when the moon follows, then
you are not alone.

Bravery, diligence, honesty, are the waters for lives,
you are family,
everybody pitches in for the same goal.
Your enthusiasm like the sun
in summer is so bright.
My heart doesn't belong to me anymore.
Since I met you
oh, how should I say
you make me feel?
I love you so much more than words can say.

In this summer dream, everything is honey, honey,
honey breath;
daylight pours down a golden river
without any name; it flows on and on,
breath bringing honey sweetness
sunbeams giving hopeful enthusiasm to life.
This was always your country, your land.
Remaining full our lives are growing together.

All over this nation high rises are going up.
Summer came filled with *living water*
shouting excitement, I am enjoying summer rains.
I pray more beautiful lives will flourish here
in the countryside, softly touching, and breathing
summer's honey breath.

What a Wonderful Watercolor Scroll?
found lines in class 8

White cranes float on the breeze
landing in apricot trees at sunset.
Going back home
smiling and singing;
the air is filled with the flower's fragrances
there is harmony in the orange sunlight.

A mother stands under an apricot tree
waiting for her son
she's anxious and worried
her shadow lengthens in the western light.
On this peaceful evening
the earth's blue tones slowly swallow the sun.

A stream silently flows along
fields, and woods into the wide river, where
a fleet of boats return from fishing.

Two cranes are whispering on a bench
apricot leaves begin falling
floating away on the water
children here smile while playing
wearing hats they've weaved out of flowers.

Leaves toss on the wind
branches are bending over full
with plush apricots ripe for harvest.
Children sing under the trees
pure delight is ringing in their laughter.
The stream flows quietly around the trees
as they stretch to receive the last light of day,
at last the earth will sleep.

One child has a sweet smile
an innocent beauty.
Leaf shapes flutter in the breeze
like decorations or rapidly beating hearts.
Pink clover cradles the golden sunbeams;
brilliant purple flowers emit their delicate scent.
The calm stream is surrounded by these colors.

"Better City Better Life"
2010 World Expo theme in Shanghai
found lines in class 3

> "I will work as hard as I possibly can to see
> what will happen." —"Homeless to Harvard"

Harmonious society
beautiful environment
friendly people,
a better city needs
everyone to make their contribution.
Some mistakes were made
on the way to happiness
science harmed our environment,
but we will care for our planet from now on.
We create miracles,
if we believe we are a global family.
The poor in Africa go through their problems
poor hands and rich hands clasping,
and wars disappear forever.

Life will be better if we protect our environment;
the more sustainable, and the more friendly
life will be if we save our natural resources.
What we save will remain for our grandchildren.
If we use our hands, we shall make
beautiful cities with more public access.

Paris, London, New York,
Hong Kong, and Shanghai
are cities leading enjoyable lives.
London is elegant;
Paris is romantic;
Hong Kong is fashionable;
New York is enthusiastic and hopeful;
and Shanghai has the World Expo.

Sweet smiles, and colorful flames
bring love to every corner of Shanghai.
Bright sunshine, and warm greetings
flow into your heart when you
give a hand to anyone who needs help.
For others and for ourselves the blue
chrome sky brings us all fresh air and happiness.

The Green
Jade Flute

An Ignorant Commune

Have they
eaten all the wild
animals on their land?
Are they
now trying to
eat all the insects?

Setting the Scene

On stage in Qufu, on the street
towards Confucius temple,

trees, shrubs, flowers, all
transplanted in curving rows,

real and surreal,
unnatural roadsides and plazas were

manipulated, controlled like
in an unending nightmare.

Natural Shape

Tyrannosaurus Rex
crouching—
head twisted to the right

ferocious jaws
stretched open
his unyielding body
prepared to pounce

a landscape rock at Jining University
an igneous stone—

clouds change shape
form a temporal wispy illusion
in transparent mist
in moonlight.

The Harvest Moon Has Risen Over

Workers in fields;
I am working
in my field
all night long
hoeing an adjective
cutting down
a weedy rhyme
walking wordings
like love over there
in rows and back
chopping a bad simile
as if it was a Canadian
thistle or pigweed.
I roll up my sleeves
and my hands get dirty
while aspen leaves flutter
on the breeze, and this
purely luminous cloud floats
past the brilliant moon.

Some Poets I Knew Then

Some poets have walked beside me
with confidence.
I've read their work.
And I've cherished their kind friendship;
most of those I've met
I thought were better than me, and others,
who may have been more popular,
whether I knew them in person
or met them through exchanged
correspondences.
Some poets I have known only
through reading their poems.

Advice for a Young, or an Old Poet

People will cheat
and mistreat you,
lie, and steal, and
I have been hoodwinked, and railroaded
many times in my life.
I will offer this sage advice.
Stand your ground.
Forgive and forget! Its better
than ranting and raving.
And pursue your goals.

On Mother's Birthday

Some serene evening
sun awash with colorful
clouds in an Asian sunset, too many
students were writing about Huck Finn.
In the back of the room
my wife wrote a letter, or
sometimes she knitted.
I have gone a long way
searching for felicity.

By Moonlight

May and June
are beautiful
no matter
where you are.
I love it
when nature
has rebirth,
everything comes
back alive;
it's miraculous
to breathe
fresh air,
and see
the lush
green fields.
Or after a
rain storm
to walk
by moonlight.

The Road to Heaven

Was written, for children who died long ago
in China, in America, and everywhere,
as I reach the peak on mountain number nine.

Chinese Folk Dancing

Incredible feminine dancers
with thousands of arms floating up
became a living pink lotus blossom.

Dancing underneath the moonlight
was fun beside the Confucius Wall
where flashing neon lights shaped
a one-horse-power chariot with wheels
spinning backwards, and where
my wife Summer and I folk danced to
traditional jade flute music
at apricot harvest time.

Home Again:
An Epilogue

The Drexell

A well tended line
slate billiard tables
and wooden racks
cue sticks stood sentry
along the pool hall wall
blue chalk cubes in position on
manicured green felt cushioned rails.

Eight regulation tables,
or was it ten? Mr. Ashby
the owner and manager worked there.
He taught the art of the game
proper English and complex angles
needed to make *your* cue ball
kiss the red and white ball and the rails.

As I can remember it
in the late fifties The Drexell was
an establishment like those from around
the turn of the nineteenth century.

Old men behind the counter
sat at tables playing dominos.
Along the counter was every
box of cigars and brand of tobacco.

There was a soda fountain
where the grill served up
cheeseburgers and chili,
or breakfast if you came early
like I did before school.

I wrote lyrics in my head while
walking there to play
the pinball machines.
In my pocket
there were always a few nickels and dimes
from a job selling Courier newspapers
on the street corner,
or from part of my mother's
waitressing tips she had shared with me.
Always I had loose change
for movies, ice cream and pinball.

Those pinball machines
were right inside the back door
and I loved the game.
You put your nickel in
and if you were good
you could win free games.

Mr. Ashby wore a gentleman's mustache
and was one of the men I admired most
at a distance, while I was struggling
to grow up without a dad.

George, his youngest son, played the cornet;
he was my age, and in my fourth grade class.
Our friendship was divided
like breaking bread and looking up . . . .

Three consecutive summers we peddled
a tandem bicycle we'd rented, 20 miles
through emerald corn fields
across the Illinois prairie to Franklin
and home. But mostly the time that
we spent together was spent playing billiards,
trying to learn the game.

Gangsta Shakespeare

He wears a gold ring in his nose.
And another's in his left eyebrow.
He has a black sleeveless shirt on.
And there's a snake tattoo on his right arm.

He's bustin' rhymes here and everywhere.
And in college he's a sophomore running back.
He's goin' first this year in the NFL draft.
With 3,000 all purpose yards, he's leaving early.

And he's thumbing his nose at creative writing.

Creating a Shimmering Shifting Mosaic Pattern

Beside the trail the wide Poudre River currents
flowed and beyond that in the distance
the majestic panorama of the snowy peaks of
the Colorado Rockies continental divide.

On my right hand were the sparkling waters
of the River Ponds nature preserve.

There was a flock of big white birds
in the center of the pond.

The birds swam close together disturbing the
water, moving randomly in a close knit flock,
about thirty birds.

I couldn't tell right away
what type of birds they were.
I thought — they might be white swans pausing —
until I ran closer, and clearly
recognized their distinguished beaks.

They were large, orange and were
dipping them into the water
and raising them up full.
It was a flock of pelicans.

Although they looked all white
while they swam, churning the water
and dipping their heads,
they had very wide wing spans
and the entire underside of
their wings were black
as were their outer wing-tips.

Continuing on around the ponds,
I heard the song of the redwing black birds,
and the honking of many Canadian Geese
that were everywhere
around the water's edge.

I didn't know if the pelican flock would still be there when I
came around the other side
of the River Ponds, but I sure hoped to see
the magnificent wild birds again.

The pelicans were there as I ran
along the eastern side of the first pond.
And I was glad to see them again
even though I was farther from them.
They were relaxed, not packed in a
small group like before, and they swam
separately more spread out around the pond.

As I rounded the turn
going west on the south edge of the pond
a solitary pelican flew over me
about twenty-five feet over my head and
I paused to look at him. And I thought,

what a beautiful and graceful creature?
The bird circled me.
The bird circled me again.
I didn't know if he was looking at me,
or coming closer so that I could look at him.
I watched as he circled higher, and
farther south, then I saw another bird circling
majestically, and then I spotted
a second flock far away
up in the air . . .
circling
and circling, higher, and farther south,
in a large compact group.
As they circled their color,
the color of the entire group, kept changing
from black to white;
and back to black,
as I could see first
the underside of their wings, and then
the top white of their wings
creating a shimmering shifting
mosaic pattern.

As the other two birds joined
in that incredible pattern,
they all broke out of that group into a single line.

Going west towards the snowy mountains . . .

the last four pelicans broke away
and flew north side-by-side
together and glided directly
over me, towards the first group
that swam in the water.

I watched as the American Pelicans flew over me
and continued my slow pace running home.

Victor W. Pearn

Victor W. Pearn was born in 1950 in Jacksonville, Illinois, and began writing poems at Kaneohe Bay, Hawaii, when he was 21 years old. He attended Lincoln Land Community College, Springfield, Illinois. He was on the Dean's list and served on the Student Senate as a Senator. At the end of his freshmen year he scored high on the CLEP exam, and skipped his sophomore year, and entered the university in January as a junior.

He spent the next summer studying abroad doing his internship in Anthropology and Writing, at Madrid University. He studied Spanish culture and language, and kept a daily journal written in English about his experiences there. At the time Spain was under a dictatorship. When he returned to Springfield the Dean at the University of Illinois wanted to publish his journal, but Mr. Pearn said, "No thanks." The journal written in Spain has not yet been published.

He earned his BA from the University of Illinois, Springfield, and his English Literature MA at Colorado University, Boulder. "One Year of Grace," won the 1983 university-wide poetry contest, and was printed as the prologue in the *1984 Coloradan* by Colorado University.

He's the author of *Devil Dogs and Jarheads,* a collection of poems describing the culture of the U.S. Marine Corps during the war in Vietnam, published by Michael Cooper, at Buscainc.com. Poems from that book have been read four times by Garrison Keillor on his American Public Media broadcast, *The Writer's Almanac.*

In 2009–2010 Mr. Pearn instructed eight freshmen English classes and six sophomore writing classes, a total of 585 English majors, at Jining University located in Qufu, China. Currently, he resides with his wife Summer, where he continues writing and publishing books and poems, in Colorado.

He has written the following twelve books:

Blame it on a Lightning Bolt, MAF Press, NY, 1989

Swans Pausing, Foothills Publishing, CO, 1994

Pyromaniac, Plowman Printing House, Canada, 1995

Dancing Bears, Poetry Forum Press, PA, 1998
(These poems won Poetry Forum's national contest)

American Western Song: poems, Xlibris, PA, 2000

Devil Dogs and Jarheads, Busca, NY, 2003

Point Guard, novel, Pearn and Assoc., CO, 2006

Cryptozoology Poems, Foothills Publishing, CO, 2006

Postcard from Athens, Kindred Spirit Press, KS, 2007

Dream Season: My Brother Gary and the 1957 Ashland Panthers, biography, Pearn and Assoc., CO, 2011

Light Across the Alley, novel, Pearn and Assoc., CO, 2011

Apricot Harvest, poems, Pearn and Assoc., CO, 2012

www.ingramcontent.com/pod-product-compliance
Lightning Source LLC
Chambersburg PA
CBHW020618270326
41927CB00005B/395